Weird about Canadian Animals

Einstein Sisters

KidsWorld

D0779991

Flying squirrels have special **flaps of skin** that **stretch** from their ankles to their wrists. They act like a parachute so the squirrel can glide from tree to tree.

Flying squirrels are **nocturnal.** This means they **sleep** in the day and are **active at night.** They have **huge, bulgy eyes** so they can see in the dark.

There are **2 types** of flying squirrels in Canada—**northern** and **southern flying squirrels.**

Flying Squirrel

Narwhal

No one
is sure what
the **horn** is used for.
People used to **believe**
that the narwhal's **tusk**
was a **unicorn**
horn.

Male narwhals
have a **giant horn.**
This horn, or **tusk**, grows
out of their **upper lip.** It is
actually a **long tooth. Females**
can also grow a horn, but it
is much smaller.

Narwhals **change colour** as they get **older**. They are **bluish grey** when they are born and become **bluish black** as young whales. Adults are a **spotty grey**, and old whales are **almost white**.

These whales can live to be about **90 years old**.

Narwhal whales like to **swim upside down**.

Narwhals are whales that live in cold **Arctic waters**.

Wood Frog

Female wood frogs are **bigger** than males.

Wood frogs **live in wetlands.** They like **swamps,** wet **forests** and bogs.

Wood frogs **do not dig underground** in winter **like most frogs** do. Instead, they **hide in fallen leaves** on the ground.

When it gets really cold outside, the frog **freezes.** It **stops breathing** and its heart **stops beating.** When the weather gets warm, the frog **thaws.** It starts to breathe again, and its heart starts to beat. It can then **hop around** as usual.

Polar bears can **close** their **nostrils** when they swim.

Polar

Because of their thick fur and layer of blubber, these giant bears are more likely to be too hot than too cold. In summer, when sea ice is melting and bears are stuck on land, they will often dig dens into frozen ground, where they can lay to keep cool.

Everyone knows a **polar bear** is **white,** right? Wrong! A polar bear's **skin** is actually **black,** just like its **nose** and **tongue.** Its fur is **hollow** and has **no colour.** The white that we see is just a **trick of the light.**

Bear

The polar bear does not need to **drink** water. Its body **makes** all the water it needs when it **digests** the bear's favourite food— seal blubber.

Ocean Sunfish

This fish has **no scales**, just a **rubbery** skin that is covered in **mucus.**

This fish is most often seen **lying on its side** at the **ocean's surface.** It may be trying to **warm** itself in the **sun** or letting **sea birds** eat the **parasites** off its skin.

The **ocean sunfish** has no real tail, just a **short, rudder-like** fin called a **clavus.** With no tail, it is a very **slow swimmer,** but it can somehow **leap 3 metres** out of the water—as high as a **basketball net** is from the ground!

The ocean sunfish is the world's **biggest** bony fish. It can grow to be **bigger** than a **car**.

The **female ocean sunfish** can make **more eggs** at one time than any other **fish**, **bird**, **reptile** or **amphibian**.

Rock
Pigeon

Pigeons
have a great sense
of direction. If they are set
free in a place they don't know,
they can find their way
home again.

The only
places in the world
where the pigeon doesn't live
are the Sahara Desert,
Antarctica and the
high Arctic.

In New Zealand,
pigeons were used as the first
air mail, carrying letters from one
island to another. People had to buy
special stamps to put on the letters
before the birds were set
loose to fly.

Until their
chicks are a few
weeks old, pigeons feed
them "crop milk." This liquid
is not really milk; it is the lining
of the adult birds' crop (a pouch where
food is stored before it gets digested). The
chicks stick their beak into the parents'
open mouth, and the parents burp
up the crop milk for the chicks
to swallow.

Sea Lamprey

This fish
is a **parasite.**
To eat, it **attaches**
its mouth to a fish's body
and **sucks** out its **blood.** Some
big fish might be okay,
but most fish die after
being **attacked**
by a lamprey.

The **sea lamprey** is a **boneless, jawless fish.** It is shaped like an **eel**, but its mouth is a huge, **toothy circle.**

The **sea lamprey** lives in the Atlantic Ocean. It has also spread into the **Great Lakes**, where it is causing a lot of **trouble** for other fish. It has even **killed off 3 species** of fish.

Elephant Seal

Female elephant seals are about **half the size** of the **males.** They also look much different because they **don't** have a big nose.

The **elephant seal** gets its name for the **male's huge, trunk-like nose**, called a **proboscis**. The male can blow his nose up like a **balloon**; this makes his voice louder when he **yells** and makes him **scarier** to other seals that might want to **fight him**.

There are **2 types** of elephant seals—northern and southern elephant seals. **Northern** elephant seals live in the **Arctic**. The southern species lives in **Antarctica**. Northern elephant seals are **smaller** than the southern seals, but the males' **nose** is **bigger**.

These jellyfish can be dark purple or **red** to **orange**. Their tentacles are usually red or **yellow**.

Lion's Mane Jellyfish

These giant **jellyfish** live in the **Arctic Ocean** and northern regions of the **Pacific** and **Atlantic** oceans. In the **southern** part of their range, these jellyfish are only about **10 centimetres long**. The farther north they live, the **bigger** they grow.

The **lion's mane jellyfish** is the **biggest** jellyfish in the world. The **largest** one ever found had **tentacles** that were longer than a **blue whale**.

This bird is the **largest grouse** species in North America.

The male sage grouse has **air sacs** in his chest that he can blow up like a **balloon** to **impress** female grouse. He also does a **special dance** to win his **mate**.

The **sage grouse** is an **umbrella species**, which means that protecting it helps **protect** a lot of **other animals** that live in the same **habitat**.

The sage grouse **lives in** sagebrush ecosystems in **southern Alberta** and **Saskatchewan**. It is at risk of becoming **endangered** because of **habitat loss**.

Sage Grouse

The **blue whale** is the **biggest animal** that has ever lived. It is as **long** as a basketball court. Its **heart** is **bigger** than a **small car**.

Blue Whale

The blue whale eats about **40 million krill** everyday.

A blue whale **mother** produces about **200 litres** of milk every day—almost enough to **fill a bathtub** right to the top.

Star-nosed Mole

This mole can smell underwater. It **blows** out **air bubbles** then **breathes** them back in to **catch a scent.**

Star-nosed moles are **good swimmers.**

In winter, this mole's **tail swells** to **2 or 3 times** its normal size. It may be **storing fat** for times when **food** is **harder to find.**

The **star-nosed mole** is almost **blind.** It uses the **22 tentacles** on its **nose** to **feel** its way around.

Water
Strider

The **water strider** is one of the only creatures in the world that can **walk on water.** It has **special hairs** on its legs that **trap air** and **push away water** so it can **skate** on top of the water rather than **floating** in it.

The water strider **cannot swim.** If it goes into the **water,** it will **drown** unless it can **crawl out** onto a nearby **rock or branch.**

This insect's **favourite foods are** dragonflies and mosquito larvae, but it will eat any **bug** that **falls into** the water.

This **little shrew** can eat **3** times its **body weight** of food **every day.**

The **short-tailed shrew** is almost **blind**. It can tell light from dark but can't see **objects**. Like a bat, it uses **sound** to move around and **find prey.**

The northern short-tailed shrew has a **poisonous bite.** Its spit has a **venom** that **paralyzes its prey.** Because of this venom, the shrew can kill **animals much bigger** than it is. It also **stores** paralyzed prey to be **eaten later.**

Northern Short-tailed Shrew

Short-horned Lizard

To **scare** away predators, a short-horned lizard can **shoot blood** out of the corner of its **eyes**. It aims for the predator's face and can hit a target standing up to 1 metre away.

It is also called the **horned toad** or **horny toad**.

In **Canada**, this lizard lives only in **southern Alberta** and **Saskatchewan**. It is **endangered**.

This lizard can also **blow itself up** like a **balloon** so that it looks **bigger** and **scarier** to any **predator** that wants to eat it.

Walrus

A walrus can sleep in the water. It has special air sacs in its chest that it can blow up like a balloon. These sacs keep the walrus' head out of the water while it sleeps. A sleepy walrus can use its tusks to anchor itself to ice so it doesn't bob around in the ocean like a cork.

A male walrus will sing to win a mate. He whistles, barks and makes bell-like sounds as he pounds his chest with his flippers to hit his air sac.

A walrus' skin is grey, but when the walrus is cold its skin looks whitish. When it's warm, the skin is more pinkish.

Plains Spadefoot Toad

The **plains spadefoot toad** lives in **hot, dry areas** of the southern Prairies. To stay cool, it **buries** itself in the **sand.** Using its **spade-like feet**, it digs **butt first** through the dry sand until it reaches the **moist layer** underneath.

When the weather gets **too hot,** this toad goes into **estivation,** which is the same as hibernation except it happens in **hot weather.** In this state, the toad **does not** need to **eat** or **drink.**

Little Brown Bat

When it is **not flying**, this bat usually **hangs by its feet.** A female giving **birth**, though, has to turn things around. She **hangs** by her **wingtips** and **catches the baby with her tail.** The baby **clings** to its mom until it is about **3 weeks old.**

If it **falls** into the **water**, this bat can **swim** short distances to **safety.**

This little bat **weighs** the same as a **loonie.** It can fit in the **palm** of a **grownup's hand.**

The **little brown bat eats** up to **1000 insects** every night. It can catch prey with its **mouth**, but it also catches insects with its **wingtips** or **tail** and tosses them into its **mouth.**

Porcupine

A **scared** porcupine will make its **quills** stand **straight up** and **swing its tail** back and forth. If it hits its **attacker** with its tail, the quills will **stick** in the attacker's skin. Then the attacker's **body heat** makes the **quills swell** so they are hard to **pull out**.

A porcupine **cannot shoot** its quills. The quills do **come off easily**, though, when something touches them. The porcupine **grows new quills** in place of any it has **lost**.

A **baby** porcupine, called a **porcupette**, is born with **soft quills**. About an hour later, the quills become **spiky**.

Porcupines have **orange teeth.**

Porcupines are **great swimmers.** Their **quills** are **hollow** and help them **float.**

The **burrowing owl** nests in a **hole** in the ground. It can dig its own **burrow**, but it would rather use one **already dug** by a **ground squirrel** or **skunk**.

This owl **lines** the opening of its burrow with **cow** or **deer poo** to attract its favourite prey—**dung beetles.**

Though it **can fly,** this small owl **often runs** after its prey.

The burrowing owl **hunts** both day and night. In the **day** it hunts mostly **insects.** At **night** it hunts more **mammals.**

Burrowing Owl

Parasitic Jaeger

This **seabird** is the **pirate of the sky.** It follows other birds, like **puffins,** that have caught fish and **steals** the fish right out of their **beaks,** or **snatches** it from their **feet.**

It will also **bully** a bird that has **just eaten** until the bird **throws up.** Then it **swoops** down and **eats** the **food** the other bird **puked up.**

This bird is also called the **arctic skua.** In summer, it **nests** on the **arctic tundra.**

Mormon
Cricket

Mormon crickets usually eat **plants**, but sometimes they eat **each other**. When these crickets **swarm**, one might eat another that gets **too close** to it.

One cricket can eat the **whole body** of another cricket the same size. Of animals that **chew their food**, it is the **only one** that can eat that much **all at once**.

Mormon crickets are not actually crickets—they are **katydids**.

They can be **brown, black, red, purple** or **green**.

When its **parents** go to find food, a **northern fulmar chick** is left behind in the nest. To **protect itself**, the chick **spits** up a **smelly oil** at any attackers. A **4-day-old chick** shoots its **spit** up to **half a metre.**

The **smelly oil** is like food for the chicks. It **slows down** their **digestion** so they can **stay full longer** while their **parents are at sea.**

Fulmar eggs also have a **weird smell,** perhaps so that **predators** won't want to **eat them.**

Northern Fulmar

Virginia Opossum

The **Virginia opossum** is the only marsupial in **North America.**

An opossum **mother** often carries her **babies** on her **back.**

This little creature has **50 teeth**— more than any other **land mammal.**

When the opossum feels **threatened,** it **plays dead.** It lays on its side with its **eyes half open** and releases a **green, slimy ooze** from its butt that smells like **rotten meat.** Once the **danger** has passed, the opossum gets up and **wanders away.**

Both male and
female pronghorns
have horns.

Pronghorn

The **pronghorn** is the fastest land animal in North America. It is the second fastest animal **in the world**, after the **cheetah**. Unlike the cheetah, the pronghorn can run at **top speed** for great **distances**. The **cheetah** can only sprint in a **short burst** before it gets tired.

Pronghorns **won't jump fences.** Instead they **scoot under** the bottom line of wire. **Special fences** have been built in parts of **Alberta** to make sure pronghorns can go **under them safely.**

Until they are **fast** enough to run with the **herd**, pronghorn **fawns** stay **hidden** in the tall grass.

American Bittern

This bird has a **loud booming call.** Because it is so well **camouflaged,** you are more likely to **hear** a bittern than **see one.**

Some of the bittern's **favourite foods** are **fish, eels, snakes** and insects.

The **American bittern** lives in **marshy** areas or **wet meadows** with **reeds.** To **hide** from predators, this bird **stretches** its body up, tips its head back and **sways** back and forth, like grass **blowing in the wind.** The **stripes** on its neck blend in with the **reeds.**

Striped Skunk

The **skunk** is **famous** for its **smelly spray.** The spray comes from **special glands** in the **skunk's butt.** This little stinker has **great aim** and usually goes for an attacker's eyes.

One of the skunk's **favourite foods** is **hairy caterpillars.** The caterpillar's **spines** can be **toxic** and can poke the skunk's **mouth** and **throat,** so the skunk **rolls the caterpillar** on the ground to **rub off** the spines **before eating it.**

Before it **sprays**, the skunk **raises its tail** straight up as a **warning**.

Baby skunks can **spray** by the time they are 3 weeks old.

If a turkey vulture **feels threatened**, it will **puke up** its last meal. It **makes sure** the pile of puke is **between** itself and its attacker so the **smell** will hopefully **drive the predator away.** After the bird has puked, it **weighs less,** so it can **take off faster** from the ground if it needs to **fly away.**

This **bird** has **no feathers** on its **face** so it can stay **cleaner** while it eats **rotting meat.**

The turkey vulture is a **scavenger**. It **doesn't kill** its prey; it eats animals that are **already dead**.

Grey
Treefrog

The grey treefrog has **toe pads** that act like suction cups. It can **climb up** trees, leaves, walls...**pretty much anything.** Each toe pad is **sticky** to help the frog **cling** to what it is climbing.

This frog can have **warty green, grey** or **brown skin,** and it can **change the colour** of its skin to **match its surroundings.**

The **grey treefrog** is **1 of 7** species of treefrog in **Canada.**

Northern Walkingstick

The **northern walkingstick** looks like a **small branch** with **twigs**. To hide from **predators**, this insect **sways back and forth** so it looks like a branch **blowing in the breeze.**

Birds, bats and many types of reptiles eat this insect.

If this insect **falls off a plant**, it **lies still** on the ground until **night.** Once it is dark, the walkingstick slowly **climbs back onto its plant.**

Sea otters do not have a layer of **blubber** to keep them warm. Instead they have really thick fur.

The sea otter loves to eat shellfish like oysters, mussels and crabs. It **holds** the shellfish on its **belly** and uses a **rock** to **hammer** through the hard shell. It sometimes **keeps a rock** tucked into its **armpit** until its **next meal.**

Sea Otter

A mother otter often carries her baby on her **belly** to keep it out of the **cold water.**

© 2014 KidsWorld Books
Printed in China

All rights reserved. No part of this work covered by the copyrights hereon may be reproduced or used in any form or by any means—graphic, electronic or mechanical—without the prior written permission of the publishers, except for reviewers, who may quote brief passages. Any request for photocopying, recording, taping or storage on information retrieval systems of any part of this work shall be directed in writing to the publisher.

The Publisher: KidsWorld Books

Library and Archives Canada Cataloguing in Publication

Weird facts about Canadian animals / Einstein Sisters.

ISBN 978-0-9938401-0-4 (pbk.)

1. Animals—Canada—Miscellanea—Juvenile literature. I. Einstein Sisters, author

QL219.W43 2014   j591.971   C2014-904202-7

Cover Images: Front cover: belovodchenko/Thinkstock. *Back cover:* flying squirrel, KarenUpNorth/Thinkstock; narwhal, Andreas Meyer/Thinkstock.
Background Graphics: abstract swirl, hakkiarslan/Thinkstock, 5, 7, 29, 31, 39, 43, 47, 57, 61; abstract background, Maryna Borysevych/Thinkstock, 13, 25, 33, 45, 49, 51, 59; pixels, Misko Kordic/Thinkstock, 2, 8, 10, 14, 19, 20, 30, 34, 36, 38, 41, 42, 54, 56.
Photo Credits: Flickr: Brian Snelson, 10–11; Gilles Gonthier, 28, 29; gordonramsaysubmissions, 24, 25; papertygre, 19; Paul and Jill, 30–31; USFWS Headquarters, 37; USFWS Pacific, 15. Thinkstock: Andreas Meyer, 4–5; Arsty, 14; Bernd Schmidt, 8; ca2hill, 6–7, 59; Comstock Images, 54; Design Pics, 34–35; Dgwildlife, 46–47; FiledIMAGE, 16–17; gdbeeler, 20; Hemera Technologies, 47; HowardPerry, 32–33; Jacob Hamblin, 44–45; John Alves, 62–63; Jupiterimages, 9; KarenUpNorth, 2; KarSol, 60–61; KathyKeifer, 58–59; LowellRichards, 63; Lynn_Bystrom, 38; MikeLane45, 42–43; MR1805, 22–23; Musat, 56–57; PaulReevesPhotography, 12–13; Philip Robertson, 53; Purestock, 18; rixonline, 38–39; Robert Blanchard, 57; Sidney Cromer, 50–51; sodapix sodapix, 16; SteveByland, 52–53; stevstep08, 40; thomasmales, 26–27; Tom Brakefield, 3; Tom Tietz, 21, 51.

We acknowledge the financial support of the Government of Canada.
Nous reconnaissons l'appui financier du gouvernement du Canada.

Funded by the Government of Canada
Financé par le gouvernement du Canada | Canadä

PC: 38